Samuel Crocker Cobb

An historical address delivered on the occasion of the

centennial celebration at Boston, Massachusetts

July 4, 1883

Samuel Crocker Cobb

An historical address delivered on the occasion of the centennial celebration at Boston, Massachusetts
July 4, 1883

ISBN/EAN: 9783337203177

Printed in Europe, USA, Canada, Australia, Japan

Cover: Foto ©ninafisch / pixelio.de

More available books at **www.hansebooks.com**

1783—1883.

The Massachusetts Society of the Cincinnati.

———•———

AN HISTORICAL ADDRESS

DELIVERED ON THE OCCASION

OF

THE CENTENNIAL CELEBRATION

AT BOSTON, MASSACHUSETTS,

JULY 4, 1883,

BY SAMUEL C. COBB,

PRESIDENT.

BOSTON:

PRINTED BY ORDER OF THE SOCIETY.

1883.

At the Centennial Dinner of the MASSACHUSETTS SOCIETY of THE CINCINNATI, given at Boston July 4, 1883, on motion of Mr. WILLIAM H. SAVAGE, seconded by Mr. DANIEL C. LILLIE, it was unanimously voted that the Historical Address delivered this day by the President, be printed, and that a copy thereof be sent to each member of the Society.

Attest:

DAVID G. HASKINS, JR.,

Assistant Secretary.

ADDRESS.

BROTHERS OF THE CINCINNATI:

THE pleasant duty devolves upon me of welcoming you, which I do most cordially, to this reunion of the MASSACHUSETTS CINCINNATI.

Besides the pleasures that are wont to attend these annual gatherings, it is our privilege to-day to perform a most grateful service, in taking note of the fact that this honored Institution has recently completed the first century of its existence. I am sure you would hardly forgive me, — indeed, I should consider myself to be remiss in the performance of my duty, — if I did not take occasion at this time to glance briefly at some of the facts and incidents connected with the history of this Society.

There is in our archives a paper in the well-known handwriting of General Henry Knox, with this indorsement: "Rough Draft of a Society to be formed by the American Officers, and to be called 'The Cincinnati.'" It is dated "West Point, April 15, 1783." It covers eight foolscap pages, and exhibits various erasures and interlineations, but is in substance the same as the present Institution. The discovery of this interesting document, the existence of which was long unknown, settled the question which had sometimes been asked as to who was the founder of the Cincinnati?

The idea of forming such an organization was at first supposed to have been suggested by Baron Steuben, as stated in Judge Burke's famous pamphlet, entitled " Considerations on the Order or Society of the Cincinnati ; " but this is shown to be an error by the Baron's letter to Knox of Nov. 11, 1783, in which, referring to Burke's assertion, he says, " He makes me author and grand-master of the Cincinnati; this is whipping you over my shoulders." [1] Brigadier-General Huntington, of Connecticut, who was one of the committee to consider and report upon the original draft of the Institution, probably had a hand in revising and shaping the instrument as finally adopted.

A glance at the condition of affairs at the close of the Revolution — a most critical period of our national history — is essential to a proper understanding of the motives and objects of the founders of the Society.

During the winter of 1782–83, the American forces lay encamped at Newburg, on the banks of the Hudson. The war was over, and independence secured; but the country was exhausted, and the outlook anything but promising. The army felt that its dissolution was imminent, and that very soon its members were to

[1] Steuben's letter is among the Knox Papers in the library of the New England Historic Genealogical Society.

be dismissed forever from the service of their country, with no other resources than such as chance or their own private means might afford. Congress, no longer the illustrious body that had once riveted the attention of the civilized world, and wielded autocratic power, — Congress was now so destitute of influence as to be wholly unable to provide for the payment of the troops, then largely in arrears; all it could do was to recommend to the different States to permit the money for national purposes to be levied : a recommendation was regarded or not, as the case might be. All this was well understood by the army. The members felt that they would never get their money unless some definite arrangement were made before the organization was disbanded. To add to their irritation, the public prints made strenuous opposition to granting pensions for military services, — an opposition prompted by those prudent patriots who had stayed at home during the war, but who now, when danger was over, fearlessly came to the front. Congress afterward issued certificates for five years' pay, in lieu of the half-pay for life that it had previously granted. These the more needy of the soldiers were obliged to part with at a ruinous discount. Often, on reaching home, the war-worn veteran had nothing to show for his long service but his ragged uniform and his honorable scars.

Poverty had made sad work among these men. Poorly paid, they had as a general rule been compelled to depend to a greater or less extent upon their own scanty resources. Their wives and daughters (and we should never lose sight of this fact), — the women of the Revolution, — had borne a part in the toils and sacrifices of the long and arduous struggle for independence with a patient heroism no whit inferior to the more active valor of husbands and brothers. Not only did they encourage and stimulate the men in the performance of patriotic duties, but often, besides discharging their own household labors, they did the men's work in the cultivation of the farm.

"The situation of the officers," writes Washington to Hamilton, March 12, 1784, "I do believe is distressing in the extreme. It is affirmed to me that a large proportion of them have no better prospect before them than a jail, if they are turned loose without liquidation of accounts, and an assurance of that justice to which they are so worthily entitled."

It is not wonderful, therefore, that a spirit of disaffection pervaded the ranks. An anonymous writer [1] gave forcible and eloquent expression to this feeling in a paper distributed throughout the camp, in which it was proposed that the army should relinquish the service in a body if the war continued; or, in case of peace, that they should still retain their arms, in defiance of civil authority. This paper produced intense excitement.

Impressive and critical as was the exigency, however, Washington was fully equal to its requirements. Calling the officers together, he counselled moderation in a dignified and patriotic speech, calmed the general agitation, and restored order and discipline. As he put on his spectacles to read his address he said, "You see, gentlemen, that I have not only grown gray but blind in your service." This incident, simple as it was,

---

[1] Major John Armstrong.

produced a powerful effect. " Without this scene," wrote Major Shaw to a friend, " I should never have known to what heights human nature was capable of attaining." [1]

I well remember hearing the late Rev. David Smith, D. D. (a member of this Society who died in 1862), give a graphic account of a visit that he made to the encampment of the Revolutionary army on the Hudson, just before the close of the war. His father, Captain Ebenezer Smith, came home on a short furlough, and David accompanied him on his return to the camp, being at that time scarcely sixteen years of age.

He reached West Point in time to be an eye-witness of the last review of troops made by the illustrious Commander-in-Chief at that place. The beneficent countenance and majestic presence of General Washington, as he appeared on that occasion, and the steady marching and soldierly bearing of the troops as they passed in review, made an impression upon the boy so vivid and thrilling, that the scene ever afterward, he said, seemed to him to be a present reality, and could never be effaced from his memory. He remained near headquarters till the army was disbanded; and while there he frequently saw General Washington and his associates-in-arms.

At last for the army the hour of parting struck. Old comrades who side by side, during all those years, had fought and bled, sometimes pinched by hunger and poverty to the utmost limit of human endurance, were now to separate, not knowing if they ever should meet again on earth, or what fate might have in store for them

[1] Journal of Samuel Shaw, with a memoir by Josiah Quincy, p. 105.

in the unknown future. It must be remembered that
these men thus remanded to the farm or workshop had
lost their taste for the arts of peace and their skill in
cultivating them, and with their meagre resources they
naturally viewed the coming struggle for existence
with melancholy forebodings.

Hear what Judge Burke, the ablest opponent of the
Cincinnati Society, says of these men. "It must be
remembered," says Burke, " that a series of hardy, gallant, and splendid actions, through a fierce and desperate conflict, their toils and sufferings, and their patience
under them, and, above all, the glorious success which
crowned the whole, have rendered the officers of the
American Army the most renowned band of men that
this day walk on the face of the globe." [1]

Although these men had secured the independence of
their country, they well knew that she was too poor to
do anything for them; and that if they or their children should thereafter be in need, it must be to their
comrades that they would have to look for help.

This was the situation when Knox, who had long
cherished the idea, proposed the formation of the
Society of the Cincinnati.

The desire to possess honorary. distinctions has
shown itself from the earliest times, and among
nations strongly dissimilar; and to be able to wear
them on the person as evidence of valuable service to
one's country has always been an honorable object of
ambition. The " button " of the Mandarin, the " fleece "
of the Spanish grandee, and the " garter " of the Eng-

---

[1] Considerations on the Order or Society of the Cincinnati.

lish knight are badges of distinction equally prized and coveted. The sentiment which prompts the bestowal of these incentives to exertion lies deep in the foundations of our nature. The recognition of meritorious service has been made use of by every government that could maintain pretensions to civilization; and to-day these incentives to nobler effort prevail throughout the civilized world.

On the 10th of May, 1783, a meeting of the general officers, and of one officer from the line of each regiment, was held at the cantonment of the army to consider the subject of the proposed association. Baron Steuben presided; and upon the favorable report of a committee consisting of Generals Knox, Hand, and Huntington, and Captain Shaw, three days later, at the headquarters of the brave old Baron (known since as the Verplanck manor, near Fishkill), the Institution of the Society of the Cincinnati was with great unanimity adopted.

The leading objects of the Society are thus stated in this instrument: "To perpetuate the remembrance of the achievement of national independence, as well as the mutual friendships which have been formed under the pressure of common danger, and in many instances cemented by the blood of the parties, — the officers of the American Army do hereby in the most solemn manner associate, constitute, and combine themselves into one society of friends, to endure as long as they shall endure, or any of their eldest male posterity, and, in failure thereof, the collateral branches who may be judged worthy of becoming its supporters or members."

Though smarting under their country's neglect

these patriotic men did not lose sight of her welfare. In this same instrument they declare it to be "their unalterable determination to promote and cherish between the respective States that union and national honor so essentially necessary to the happiness and the future dignity of the American Empire." It is a source of just pride that our Society, originating as it emphatically did in merit alone, should also have so valid a claim to perpetuity as is contained in this patriotic declaration. In this direction it can still be useful, and the fundamental principles upon which it rests should never be departed from.

Officers were eligible to membership who had served for three years, or to the end of the war, or who had been left out on the several reductions of the army, upon contributing one month's pay to the treasury of the respective State societies, the interest of this fund to be applied to the relief of the indigent widows and orphans of deceased members.

The General Society was to be divided into State societies, and it was to meet triennially on the first Monday in May. The triennial meeting is composed of the officers of the General Society, and a delegation of not more than five members from each State. There have been thirty-five meetings of the General Society during the century, besides those supposed to have taken place between 1811 and 1829, of which no record exists. Only temporary officers were chosen at the first meeting, as follows: Washington, President; General Knox, Secretary; and General McDougal, Treasurer. A little later, the eagle, the beautiful insignia of the order, was designed by Major l'Enfant, an accomplished engineer and draughtsman.

A number of prominent French officers who had
aided us in achieving our independence were constituted members of the Society. The French king, as a
special mark of favor, permitted them to appear at court
with the new decoration, the only foreign badge previously suffered to be worn there being that of the Golden
Fleece. The Society was held in high honor among
the French officers, and its membership was eagerly
sought by them. The terrible revolution which swept
away every vestige of rank and title in France made
sad havoc among them, and brought to the guillotine
D'Estaing, Custine, Lauzun, De Broglie, Dillon, and
others who had earned and worn the much-coveted
decoration. The especial distinction accorded to the
order by Louis XVI. was acknowledged by his successors as long as royalty held sway in France. In
Russia it has received special recognition from the
Czar; and in England the badge of the order is recognized by the Lord Chamberlain as a passport to court
ceremonials. Our Society is more generally recognized
abroad than any other American organization. At
home, many prominent men have been among its
members.

One feature of the Institution — the hereditary succession of its members — alarmed the friends of the
new republic, then at the beginning of its experimental
stage, and provoked hostile criticism from all quarters.
The ablest of its opponents was Judge Burke, of South
Carolina. The gifted Mirabeau also, afterward the
impassioned orator of the French National Assembly,
uttered this solemn warning: "In less than a century this institution, which draws a line of separation

between the descendants of the Cincinnati and their
fellow-citizens, will have caused so great an inequality
that the country which now contains none but citizens
perfectly equal in the eye of the constitution and of the
law, will consist altogether of two classes of men, —
Patricians and Plebeians."[1]

How ridiculous this prediction seems to us, and how
completely was it falsified by the event! Yet such
was the sensitiveness of popular feeling upon this
subject at that day that these and similar forebodings,
absurd as they now appear, produced a profound
impression all over the country.

That such ideas should be entertained by persons
living under monarchical governments, and unfamiliar
with the genius of our people, is not strange; the wonder is that they should have been shared by some of
the most enlightened of our own statesmen. Jefferson,
Jay, the Adamses, even the sagacious Franklin, were
among those who believed that the Society was laying
the foundation of a new order of nobility. The State
of Rhode Island threatened to disfranchise such of its
citizens as were members of the Cincinnati; but, notwithstanding the assertion of several writers that she
did deprive them of citizenship, no such step was actu-
ally taken by her, nor by any other State. McMaster,
the latest writer upon this portion of our history, not
only repeats but magnifies this error, for he tells us
that "the officer who subscribed to its laws laid down
in many States his rights of citizenship."[2]

---

[1] Considerations on the Order or Society of the Cincinnati, p. 22.

[2] McMaster's History of the People of the United States, vol. i.
p. 168.

Here in Massachusetts, a committee of both Houses of the Legislature reported, March 25, 1784, that the association was "unjustifiable, and, if not properly discountenanced, dangerous to the peace, liberty, and safety of the United States in general, and this commonwealth in particular." No action, however, was taken by the Legislature, and the excitement eventually subsided.

So strong indeed was the public sentiment against the Society in our own State at that time, that even Knox its founder, and Jackson his bosom friend, stanch supporters of the order as they were, were for a time constrained to abstain from wearing their badges;[1] and General Heath, then a candidate for senatorial honors, and fearing for the result, wrote on the eve of the election to the Secretary-General to erase his name from the Society's list of members.[2]

Knowing as we do the purity of the motives that actuated the founders of our Society, and the patriotism and beneficence that have marked its whole career; and knowing, too, the utter impossibility of founding here, even had they desired to do so, an aristocratic and privileged class, — knowing all this, one can hardly repress a smile at the wide-spread alarm and apprehension excited by the wise, perfectly simple, and proper method devised by the Society for continuing its existence.

[1] See Winthrop Sargent's article in the "North American Review" for October, 1852.

[2] General Heath paid his money, but never met with the Society. See "Heath's Memoirs," pp. 380–82. Life of Samuel Adams, by S. A. Welles, vol. iii. p. 204.

No one now thinks of questioning the wisdom of this method. The fact of its adoption by that patriotic body of men known as the "Loyal Legion," whose task it was to preserve that which our original members had contributed so largely to secure, — this fact is of itself a sufficient commentary on the judgment and good sense of the founders of the Cincinnati in establishing such a rule, however contrary it might then have been to current popular sentiment.

The first General Meeting of the Cincinnati, after the disbanding of the army, took place at the City Tavern in Philadelphia, in May, 1784. At the suggestion of Washington, and in deference to the strong and general sentiment of the country, it recommended to the State societies the abolition of the obnoxious provision in the Institution. By this timely action the opposition was silenced, and the storm hushed. After the adoption of the Federal Constitution, warfare against the Society ceased. As, however, the proposed alteration in the Institution never was agreed to by the State societies, that instrument remains to this day unaltered in this respect. At this meeting in Philadelphia the first regular officers of the Society were chosen. Washington was of course named President-General; General Gates was elected Vice-President-General; and General Knox, Secretary-General. Since its formation the presiding officers of the Society have been as follows: George Washington, Alexander Hamilton, Charles Cotesworth Pinckney, Thomas Pinckney, Aaron Ogden, Morgan Lewis, William Popham, Henry A. S. Dearborn, and Hamilton Fish. Four of the nine

have been from New York, and all but two were
Revolutionary officers.

With regard to the admission of new members, various rules have from time to time been adopted, and
there is, — unfortunately, as I believe, — no uniformity
of action in the different State societies. Since 1792,
our Society has elected its members by ballot, and in
1801 it adopted the rule of electing no person under
twenty-one years of age. The principle of limiting
membership to a single individual of the same line
prevails uniformly in Massachusetts, and, I think, in
Pennsylvania; while South Carolina admits all male
descendants, at least in the same degree of blood. In
Maryland, also, different degrees of the same stock in
the line of descent, as father and son, are admitted
together.

In all the societies from the beginning, a brother or
a nephew of an original member was eligible; and
direct male descendants, through female collateral
lines, have, upon failure of original male lines, been
made admissible, in preference to kinsmen more re-
mote. The admission of nephews has been extended
in Massachusetts and New York to one claiming
through a sister of an original member. In 1822 the
first and only instance occurred in Massachusetts of the
choice of a cousin and nearest male relative to succeed
a deceased member (William Lyman, now deceased, in
that year succeeding his cousin James W. Lyman). The
honorary membership in our Society has been limited
to three, — William H. Prescott, in 1845; Dr. John C.
Warren and Daniel Webster in 1847.

A recent rule of our Society permits a deviation from the succession of the heir male if, for satisfactory reasons, another be chosen. But upon the decease of the person so preferred, the membership reverts to the heir male of the original member.

In 1799 the South Carolina society voted to admit to membership *all* the sons and *all* the male descendants of original members, whether such descendants derived through a male or female branch, or of such officers as having served with reputation died during the war, or who having been entitled to become members died within six months after the army was disbanded, who might be judged worthy, provided three fourths of a legal quarterly meeting were in his favor, and upon the payment of thirty dollars. They also voted to admit, on a three-fourths vote and one month's pay, officers who had served six years in the army or navy of the United States, or who after three years' service had been deranged by act of Congress.[1] This action of the South Carolina branch seems clearly to be a direct violation of the organic law of the Society. No notice has been taken of it, however, by the General Society.

I am not informed of the rules of other State societies, now in force, in regard to the admission of members; but I think the records will show that the Massachusetts State society. has adhered more rigidly in this respect to the spirit of the original institution, from its beginning to the present time, than have the other State societies.

By the action of the General Society in 1854, the

[1] See letter from the South Carolina Society, dated May 23, 1799, in the archives of the Massachusetts Society.

door of admission to membership was opened to the
male descendants of such officers of the army or navy
as might have joined it originally, but who failed so to
do ; to those who resigned with honor or left the service with reputation ; and also to the male collateral
relatives of any officer who died in service without
leaving issue. It was further provided that the male
descendants of those who were members of State societies which had been dissolved, might be admitted into
existing societies upon such terms as these societies
might think proper to prescribe. This measure has had
the effect to increase the membership of the Society,
which had previously been gradually diminishing.

From the records of our State society I glean a few
items of more than ordinary interest. Its first meeting
was held at the cantonment of the Massachusetts line,
near Newburg, on the 9th of June, 1783, three weeks
after the formation of the General Society ; its subse-
quent meetings have all been held in Boston. General
Patterson presided ; one hundred and fifty members
were in attendance, and the following named officers
were chosen : President, Major-General Benjamin Lincoln ; Vice-President, Major-General Henry Knox ;
Secretary, Colonel John Brooks ; Treasurer, Colonel
Henry Jackson ; Assistant-Treasurer, Captain Benjamin
Heywood.

At a special meeting on the 11th of April, 1787, a
standing committee was organized. It was to meet
monthly to examine the claims of candidates for admission ; to distribute aid from its funds to beneficiaries ;
and to transact all other business of the Society. This

committee was subsequently enlarged, and now holds its stated meetings in March and November of each year.

In 1788–89 our State society lost some valuable members, who emigrated to the Northwestern Territory, where, under the lead of Generals Rufus Putnam and Benjamin Tupper, they founded at Marietta the first white settlement in Ohio. Among these enterprising pioneers were Colonels Sprout and Stacey, Major Oliver, Captains Nathaniel Cushing, Nathan Goodale, Zebulon King, Robert Bradford, Jonathan Stone, Huffield White, and Jonathan Haskell. These gentlemen afterward formed a branch society, and applied for their portion of the Society's funds. The request was refused as incompatible with the terms of the Institution itself, and as establishing a dangerous precedent. The capital fund has ever been regarded as a sacred trust by the Society, " to endure as long as they shall endure, or any of their eldest male posterity, and, in failure thereof, the collateral branches who may be judged worthy."

On the 10th of September, 1789, our State society was entertained on board the French fleet then in Boston Harbor, commanded by the Marquis de la Gallissonière, a member of the French Society, and on the twenty-fourth the French officers were in return the Society's guests at Concert Hall. This was a grand affair ; the hall was gayly decorated, and a full band was in attendance.

In this year occurred also President Washington's visit to Boston. He was waited on by the Society at his quarters in the building which until quite recently stood on the corner of Tremont and Court streets. The occasion was one of deep interest, six years having elapsed since their parting with their beloved commander-in-chief. An address was made by Vice-President Eustis, to which the President made a feeling and eloquent reply.

Another of these pleasant reunions occurred in 1817, when President Monroe, the second chief magistrate taken from the ranks of the Cincinnati, came to Boston. He made the Exchange Coffee House his headquarters, and received a congratulatory address from the Society.

But the most memorable of all the occasions that brought the veterans of our State society together occurred in 1824, when Lafayette, after forty years' absence, revisited our shores as the guest of the nation. Probably no one has ever received a more enthusiastic reception than that accorded upon this occasion to the "hero of two hemispheres." From the balcony of the mansion yet standing at the corner of Park and Beacon streets, with Brooks and Eustis, in their old continental uniforms, on either side of him, the distinguished visitor saw the troops and the procession pass in review. A committee of the Society called upon Lafayette at the residence of Governor Eustis in Roxbury, before his entrance into Boston. They were anxious to offer him their congratulations at the earliest moment, and to bid him welcome to the land they had unitedly struggled to defend. A few days after his arrival, the whole Society waited on him, and addressed him through their President. The General, in reply, expressed his thanks and gratification at being permitted to revisit his surviving companions of the Revolutionary Army, to whom he tendered his "grateful thanks and constant love." While in Boston, the Massachusetts Cincinnati again assembled to offer him a tribute of affection, and their meeting was deeply interesting. His venerable associates-in-arms were in tears when he addressed them, and he appeared highly affected by the interview. Lafayette's visit has a special interest for this Society, as it was made the occasion for Brooks and Eustis, brothers-in-arms, to bury an old animosity.

When in 1826 the fiftieth anniversary of the Declaration of Independence was celebrated, twenty of the old Revolutionary veterans, most of whom were over seventy years of age, assembled. One of them had not attended a meeting of the State society for forty years. We can well imagine that their greetings were warm, their reminiscences of the past abundant, and that their expressions of pleasure at being permitted once more to meet their old comrades, and to see the country for which they had fought and bled in so happy and prosperous a condition, were deep and heartfelt.

On Nov. 21, 1881, the descendants and representatives of Lafayette, Rochambeau, Noailles, and others of the gallant Frenchmen who aided us in our war for independence, were welcomed to Boston by the President of our State society, in the name of the Massachusetts Cincinnati.

For six consecutive years, beginning with 1787, orations were delivered before the Society on the 4th of July of each year. The orators were Colonel John Brooks, Colonel William Hull, Dr. Samuel Whitwell,

Colonel William Tudor, Dr. William Eustis, and Thomas Edwards. The first four were delivered at the Old Brick Meeting-house, and were printed. The last two were given in the Stone Chapel. On these occasions the Society marched in procession, accompanied by the officiating clergyman, to and from the " Bunch of Grapes " tavern to the meeting-house. The reverend gentleman opened the services with prayer, and afterward dined with the Society.

Our first annual meeting was held July 4, 1784, at the " Bunch of Grapes " tavern. This then famous hostelry, kept at that time by Colonel Marston, and afterward by Mrs. Lobdell, stood at the corner of State and Kilby streets, the present site of the New-England National Bank. After 1789, the annual festive reunions of the Society were usually held at Concert Hall, the last of these occurring in 1846. From 1848 to 1860 the Society met and dined at the United States Hotel. Since that period its meetings have been held at the Parker House.

At the earlier anniversaries of the Society the cocked hat and knee breeches and the small sword were worn. The hair carefully powdered and brought down to a pigtail claimed no small share of attention, and constituted an important feature in the costume. Old comrades met and talked over the past, recalling their varied experiences of the camp, the march, and the battle-field. Conviviality was apt to be carried to excess in those days, and it was not likely to be unduly restrained by old campaigners on the anniversary day of the nation they had helped to found.

Apropos of this now obsolete feature of our annual

gatherings was the toast of Major .Jackson, an old artilleryman. Said the Major: " May we not over-charge our old pieces, and never heat them hotter than they were at Monmouth." This is said to have been a " palpable hit."

Some of these scarred veterans present at these social reunions had served from Bunker Hill to York-town. Their talk was of the retreat through New Jersey and the night-march to Trenton, the destitution and misery of Valley Forge, the heat and dust of Monmouth, the storming of Stony Point under the lead of " Mad Anthony," the treason of Arnold, the capture and execution of Major André, and the decisive events of Saratoga and Yorktown.

The dinners — and they were good and substantial repasts — cost each member four shillings, equal to two thirds of a dollar; the wine, which was an "extra," two shillings : this was in 1789. The Master of Ceremonies was directed to call for the bill before sunset, — perhaps to avoid an extra charge for candles!

Since 1794, the cost of the annual dinner has been defrayed from the funds of the Society. The regular toasts were originally thirteen in number ; but as State after State came into the Union, their number correspondingly increased. They were usually of a patriotic character. One, which has never been omitted, is drunk standing and in silence, — " To the memory of Washington."

The Antislavery sentiment of the time is revealed in a toast given soon after the Missouri Compromise Act of 1820. It was this : " Our sister States in the South : May the time soon come, when their songs of liberty shall no longer mingle with the sighing of slaves!"

After a century of existence as a Society, the question naturally arises, Has it faithfully carried out the cherished objects of its founders? That it has perpetuated and strengthened the friendships of our members does not admit of question. Especially bright and enjoyable were those rare occasions particularly noticed in our records, that brought from a distance comrades like General North (the favorite aid of Steuben), Colonel Trumbull (the painter), Colonel Nathan Rice, and John K. Smith. The descendants of the original members have cherished and know how to value this most agreeable feature of their association.

That another and much more important object has also been borne in mind, is attested by the Society's records, which show that whenever the institutions we so highly prize were threatened either by domestic or foreign foes, the members of the Society instantly came forward to sustain the cause of union and good government.

The first of these occasions, the Shays Insurrection, occurred in Massachusetts in the winter of 1786–87. Those were dark days. The old Confederacy was falling into contempt, and there seemed little hope of uniting the discordant political elements then existing into anything like a stable form of government. Advantage was taken of this state of affairs by a few desperate men, who hoped to derive some benefit from the overthrow of the State government. Notwithstanding the fact that many of the officers were still unpaid, and extremely depressed in their private circumstances, the moment the government was in danger, they rallied unanimously to its support.

The following extract from the report of a committee of the Society, composed of Generals Knox and Lincoln, Colonel Brooks and Dr. Eustis, dated Oct. 11, 1786, and which, as the records show, was unanimously adopted, speaks for itself: "Having the happiness," say the committee in their report, "to live under a government of laws and not of men, attached to that government by the strong ties of principle and habit, valuing freedom in proportion to the sacrifices they have made in her support, this Society will never tamely suffer these inestimable blessings to be wrested from their hands by foreign force, or domestic faction. The Society are interested in the preservation of the Constitution; and so long as life and its attendant blessings, so long as public faith and private credit are made the sacred objects of government, agreeably to its original institution, this Society pledge themselves to support it by every means, and by every exertion in their power."

Nor was this all. The pledge thus given was amply redeemed. Several of the Cincinnati played a most prominent part in suppressing the outbreak which quickly had attained to formidable proportions. General Lincoln headed the forces that in mid-winter marched through deep snows against it in the west. General Shepherd, with a few cannon-shot, shattered and dispersed it in the same quarter; and General Knox, then Secretary of War, was active in providing for the security of the United States arsenal at Springfield. In Bristol County the mob, confronted by the energetic and determined officer, who declared that he would "sit as a judge, or die as a general," and who would, as they well knew, keep his word, — scattered without firing a shot.

The prospect of a war with France, in 1798, called out similar assurances from the Society of loyalty and support to the government; and there can be no doubt that had the necessity arisen, their acts would not have belied their words.

In the great rebellion which divided our country on a strictly geographical line, the large majority of the Cincinnati were actively loyal. The patriotism of the sires bore legitimate fruit in the sons. Among the gallant men who upheld our country's flag in the hour of her utmost need, the descendants of the Cincinnati were everywhere conspicuous, and proved themselves worthy of their exalted origin. South of Mason and Dixon's line the Union men, though few in number, made a gallant fight to prevent the impending catastrophe; but they were completely buried beneath the fierce waves of secession which at that time overwhelmed the Southern section of our country.

One other theme presents itself in connection with our inquiry.

We have seen how the Cincinnati have responded to the calls of friendship and patriotism. What have they accomplished toward fulfilling the beneficent designs of the founders of the order?

No sooner had the Society been organized than a committee was appointed " to inquire into the situation of distressed members." It was six years, however, before the first application for relief was made.

Two years later (1791), the standing committee was empowered to grant, annually, a sum not exceeding twenty dollars to each applicant for relief. In 1796 it was voted to apply the entire interest of the Society's fund for this purpose; and that its benevolent objects might be more fully attained, the standing committee was instructed to give public notice of its meetings. It is a matter of wonder that the applications for aid were so few in the earlier days of the Society. Forty years after its establishment the number of its beneficiaries had risen to ninety; in 1847 it had decreased to fifty, and is now but half that number. In 1862 it was found expedient to adopt a rule restricting aid so as to apply it solely to our indigent members, and to the widows and orphans of said members.

The administration of the Society's finances has always been in able hands. Its past treasurers — General Jackson, Robert Williams, and William Perkins, each of whom were many ·years in office — have by their judicious management so increased the fund of the Society as to enable it to carry out the eleemosynary provision of its Institution in a most enlarged and liberal manner. While its beneficiaries in 1847 received annually on an average but about thirty dollars each, they now receive over eighty dollars each. .

.The sums contributed by original members, as appears by our books, was $13,058.15. These were paid in Continental certificates, which were probably redeemed at par.

When it is considered that not a few of these con-
tributions were made at the cost of great personal
inconvenience and even of comfort, such as we in this
day can neither understand nor appreciate, we can the
better realize the earnest interest which these men felt
in establishing this brotherhood. One instance of this
kind has come to my knowledge. An original member
of this Society, who served through the Revolutionary
war with much distinction, — a brigadier-general at its
close, — went home to poverty, and ruined in health.
He soon afterwards died. He was so much reduced in
his pecuniary circumstances that his widow was obliged
to ask help in order to defray the expense of his
burial.

Surely, a fund gathered for such uses as was that of
the Cincinnati, and representing as it did the hard-
earned and, in some instances, the only savings of the
contributors, cannot be held too dearly or guarded too
closely by those to whose care it has been committed.[1]

The amount paid from the treasury of this Society in
aid of members and their descendants to the present
time, as the records show, exceeds ninety thousand
dollars. The expenditures for annual dinners and inci-
dentals has been another and no inconsiderable item

[1] In a circular dated June, 1836, Dr. James Thacher of Plymouth calls
for the dissolution of the Society and the distribution of its funds. " Our
glorious days are gone by," says the writer, "our work is finished; not
more than twenty of our original members survive, and the time is at
hand when not an individual of the old stock will be seen at your festive
board. Our funds might add much to the comfort of the old debilitated
soldiers if divided." At the annual meeting July 4, 1836, "the subject
of dissolving the Society, as suggested by Dr. Thacher, was debated, and
on motion it was indefinitely postponed."

of expense. Notwithstanding this, we begin the new
century with our vested capital increased fully five-
fold in amount, as compared with the sum contributed
originally.

On the rolls of our Society there are many distinguished names, to a few of which it seems proper on
this occasion briefly to refer.

The army and navy are well represented by those
of Lincoln, Knox, Rufus Putnam, Patterson, Greaton,
Shepard, Tupper, Hull, Vose, Wesson, Jackson, Nicholson, and Warren of the Revolutionary period, and by
Casey, Hunt, Townsend, Davis, and Thatcher of later
date, but of no less distinction. The names of Parker,
Baylies, Cobb, and Binney have illustrated the bench
and bar; those of Eustis, Brooks, Homans, Townsend,
Hunt, Green, and Thacher have graced the medical
profession, of whom Brooks and Eustis have also worthily filled the gubernatorial chair of Massachusetts.
The pulpit has been enriched by the piety and elo-
quence of an Ingersoll, a Ballard, a Baury, and a
Wells. In this connection I cannot forbear reference
to one [1] whom it is not necessary in this presence to
name. Far distant be the day when his genial com-
panionship shall cease from among us, to gladden and
to cheer! Science and scholarship can claim Pickering, Popkin, Tudor, Bradford, Daveis, Dearborn, and
Gould. Prominent among the distinguished names
stands that of Charles Sumner, statesman, orator, and
scholar. Franklin Pierce, one of our members, was
the fourteenth President of the United States. Other

[1] The Rev. S. K. Lothrop, D.D.

honored names will readily occur to you, such as Shaw, Sever, and others; but the list is too long to be recited on this occasion, and I must leave it incomplete.

Dr. Joseph Prescott, the last survivor of the original members, and at one time Vice-President of the Massachusetts society, died at Great Barrington, Mass., in 1852. The last of the original Cincinnati, Major Robert Burnett, survived until 1854. The Massachusetts roll contains at the present time the names of only four who are sons of original members; namely, Dr. Samuel Alden, of Bridgewater; Benjamin H. Greene, of Brookline, Mass; John Edwards, of Portland, Me.; William H. Burbeck, of New London, Conn. The roll also contains the name of William Eustis, of Philadelphia, a nephew of Governor William Eustis.

Cincinnati, the "Queen City of the West," was so named by General Arthur St. Clair, in honor of this Society, of which he was a member. St. Clair, as you remember, was the first governor of the Northwestern Territory.

Of the thirteen original State societies, seven are yet in existence. Those of North Carolina and Georgia long ago ceased to have vitality. The Delaware, Connecticut, Virginia, and New Hampshire societies were dissolved in the years 1802, 1804, 1822, and 1830, respectively, the latter by the death of its last member. The Rhode Island Society was also dissolved in 1832, but has recently been revived by sons and representatives of former members now deceased. The only State societies of the Cincinnati ever incorporated were those of Pennsylvania, in 1792; Massachusetts, in 1806; and Rhode Island, in 1814.

The Massachusetts State society has always been the largest, — the three hundred and thirty-four members who originally signed its roll being now represented by ninety of their descendants; and it is believed to have held more closely to the principles and practices of the original Institution than have either of the remaining State societies, if we except that of Pennsylvania. These two societies have, as a rule, opposed all radical departures from the Institution as originally planned.

A few figures exhibit the condition of each of the State societies, and the number of its regular and honorary members, as reported recently to the Secretary-General: —

STATE SOCIETIES.	Original Members.	Present Members.	Honorary Members.	FUND.
Massachusetts	334	90	–	$53,000.00*
New York	230	57	3	22,000.00
New Jersey	110	41	9	15,000.00*
Pennsylvania	268	34	–	36,050.00
Maryland	148	22	–	5,660.00
South Carolina . . .	131	42	–	5,500.00
Rhode Island	71	29	5	1,401.23
Totals	1,292	315	17	$138,611.23

Such, in brief, Brothers, is the record of this Society during the past hundred years.

I have no need here more than to allude to the not less interesting, as well as important, history of this brotherhood, which is, and must always remain, un-

* Securities taken at par.

written. Of the life-long friendships that have been
fostered and strengthened here; of the countless and
nameless individuals who have been the recipients of
the Society's bounty; of the genuine comfort and good
cheer it has vouchsafed to all; of the inspiration to
well-doing that has gone out from these fraternal
gatherings, hallowed by all the glorious memories
and associations that belong to them, — these have
not been, under the providence of God, without their
influence in making up the sum of the good work which
this Society has accomplished; ay, and in making better men of all those who have accepted its membership
in the true spirit of its Institution.

Standing thus at the opening of the second century of this Society's existence, we have just cause
to congratulate ourselves upon the record it has
made.

Let us look forward hopefully and confidently to
the work that is before us, remembering always that
to us has been committed for the time being all the
interests, all the nobly conservative influences and
associations, of this time-honored Society.

A glorious heritage is ours; but this inheritance im-
poses upon us important duties and responsibilities,
which can be neither overlooked nor neglected if we
would prove ourselves to be worthy of it.

There is an old proverb which is to the effect that if
we would be the equals of our fathers, we should be
superior to them; that is to say, as they occupied higher
ground than those who preceded them, so, to be their
equals, we must advance our position beyond theirs.

Let us see to it that the principles of honor, of a broad patriotism, and of an unswerving devotion to duty are the cardinal principles of our action, not only as members of this brotherhood, but as citizens of this republic which our fathers helped to found, and which they looked to their descendants to preserve, to strengthen, and to make the noblest among the nations of the earth.

Then shall an influence for good go forth from this organization which shall be worthy of its founders and of their successors; an influence founded upon the everlasting principles of justice, charity, and truth, which shall be transmitted in all its strength and fulness to the generations which shall succeed us.

Esto Perpetua !

EXERCISES AT THE CENTENNIAL DINNER,

WITH

LISTS OF OFFICERS AND MEMBERS.

Delegates to the triennial meeting of the General Society of the Cincinnati, to be holden at Princeton, N. J., in May, 1884 : —

SAMUEL C. COBB.

CHARLES D. HOMANS.

FRANCIS W. PALFREY.

WINSLOW WARREN.

SAMUEL K. LOTHROP.

CENTENNIAL DINNER

AT THE PARKER HOUSE, 2 O'CLOCK, P.M.

Music by the Germania Band.

Toast-master . . . . . . DAVID G. HASKINS, Jr.

Chaplain . . The Rev. SAMUEL K. LOTHROP, D.D.

TOASTS.

I. *The Memory of Washington.* (Standing, in Silence.)

Music: " WASHINGTON'S MARCH."

II. *The Day and Year we Celebrate:* The Birthday of our Nation, and the Centennial of our Order. We honor the memory of those who declared our Independence and of those who fought for it.

Music: " HAIL COLUMBIA."

Historical Address by the President, the Hon. SAMUEL C. COBB.

Music: " THE MARSEILLAISE."

Address by the Rev. SAMUEL K. LOTHROP, D.D.

III. *The Health of our Honored President:* The last President of the first century, the first President of the second century of our Order. Long may he live in health, honor, and prosperity, to preside over the meetings of this Society !

Response, by the President.

————

IV. *The Army and Navy of the United States:* Few in number, but mighty in spirit ; worthy sons of the men, of Bunker Hill and Valley Forge, of Lake Erie, New Orleans, and Buena Vista.

Music: "The Star-Spangled Banner."

————

V. *The Clergy :* Zealous and powerful advocates of the rights of man, whether in the pulpit, the forum, or the battle-field, in 1776 or 1883.

> " Those who, regardless of an earthly prize,
> Offer their lives a double sacrifice, —
> To God for men, to men for God: that band
> Of noble men, — the Clergy of our land."

Music.

Response, by the Rev. James G. Vose, of Providence, Rhode Island.

————

VI. *The Surgeons of* 1776, 1812, 1846, *and* 1861 : Fearless messengers of mercy amidst the horrors of the battle-field ; freely shedding their own blood at their country's call ; true to-day, as in 1775, to the motto, — " Dulce et decorum est pro patriâ mori."

Music.

Response, by the Vice-President, Charles D. Homans, M.D.

————

VII. *Plymouth Rock :* The stepping-stone from mediæval traditions to modern liberty and equal rights.

" Like cleaves to like ! The wandering exiles found
A rock, firm as their wills, on which to rest;
No yielding clay, no flower-besprinkled ground,
Would suit these men, — stern, tempest-tossed, oppressed.
The gray old rock, ne'er yielding to their tread,
Stamped its own impress on the little flock;
And we, the children of the noble dead,
Still thrill with reverence for Plymouth Rock."

Music: " AMERICA."

Response, by GAMALIEL BRADFORD.

—◆—

VIII. *The Beneficiaries of the Society :* The needs of the
children only strengthen our remembrance of the
patriotic deeds of the fathers.

Response, by WINSLOW WARREN.

—◆—

IX. *Our Brethren of the other State Societies :* May the sacred ties of sympathy and love that united in their
infancy the thirteen fair sisters, bind ever closer together the seven survivors in their mature years.

Music: " YANKEE DOODLE."

Response, by the Rev. WINSLOW WARREN SEVER,
of Poughkeepsie, N. Y.

—◆—

Closing Remarks by the Toast-master.

Music: " AULD LANG SYNE."

———

[The two poetical sentiments were written for this occasion by Mrs.
Mary C. D. Watson, granddaughter of the late Hon. Charles S. Daveis,
President of the Society].

OFFICERS

GENERAL SOCIETY OF THE CINCINNATI,

ELECTED AT THE TRIENNIAL MEETING, HELD AT
CHARLESTON, S. C., 1881.

———— ◆ ————

President-General.

HAMILTON FISH,

OF NEW YORK.

Vice-President-General.

WILLIAM A. IRVINE,

OF PENNSYLVANIA.

Secretary-General.

GEORGE W. HARRIS,

OF PENNSYLVANIA.

Assistant Secretary-General.

RICHARD I. MANNING,

OF MARYLAND.

Treasurer-General.

JOHN SCHUYLER,

OF NEW YORK:

Assistant Treasurer-General.

HERMAN BURGIN,

OF NEW JERSEY.

ORIGINAL MEMBERS

MASSACHUSETTS SOCIETY OF THE CINCINNATI.

A.

Abbott, Josiah, Ensign.
Abbott, Stephen, Captain.
Adams, Henry, Regimental Surgeon.
Alden, Judah, Captain.
Allen, Nathaniel C., Captain.
Allen, Noah, Major.
Ames, Jotham, Lieutenant.
Andrews, William, Lieutenant.
Armstrong, Samuel, Lieutenant.
Ashley, Moses, Major.
Austin, John, Lieutenant.

B.

Bailey, Adams, Captain.
Bailey, Luther, Captain.
Balcom, Joseph, Lieutenant.
Baldwin, Jeduthun, Colonel.
Ballantine, Ebenezer, Surgeon's Mate.
Ballard, William H., Major.
Bancroft, James, Lieutenant.
Barlow, Joel, Chaplain.
Bassett, Barachiah, Lieut-Colonel.
Baury de Bellerive, Captain.
Baylies, Hodijah, Lieutenant-Colonel.
Benson, Joshua, Captain.
Blake, Edward, Lieutenant.
Blanchard, John, Captain.
Bowles, Ralph H., Lieutenant and
 Adjutant.
Bowman, Samuel, Lieutenant.
Bradford, Andrew, Lieutenant.
Bradford, Gamaliel, Colonel.
Bradford, Gamaliel, Lieutenant.
Bradford, Robert, Captain.
Bramhall, Joshua, Lieutenant.

Brigham, Origen, Surgeon's Mate.
Brooks, John, Lieutenant-Colonel-
 Commandant.
Brown, Ebenezer, Lieutenant.
Brown, Oliver, Captain-Lieutenant.
Bugbee, Edward, Lieutenant.
Bullard, Asa, Lieutenant.
Burbeck, Henry, Captain.
Burnham, John, Major.
Bussey, Isaiah, Captain-Lieutenant.

C.

Callender, John, Captain-Lieutenant.
Carleton, Moses, Lieutenant.
Carleton, Osgood, Lieutenant.
Castaing, Peter, Lieutenant.
Chambers, Matthew, Captain.
Chapin, Samuel, Lieutenant.
Clap, Caleb, Captain.
Clap, Joshua, Lieutenant.
Clayes, Peter, Captain.
Cobb, David, Lieutenant-Colonel-
 Commandant.
Cogswell, Amos, Captain.
Cogswell, Samuel, Lieutenant.
Cogswell, Thomas, Major.
Condy, Thomas H., Lieutenant.
Cook, David, Captain.
Cooper, Ezekiel, Captain.
Cooper, Samuel, Adjutant.
Crane, John, Colonel.
Crane, John, Regimental Surgeon.
Crocker, Joseph, Captain.
Crowley, Florence, Lieutenant.
Cushing, Nathaniel, Captain.
Cushing, Thomas, Lieutenant.

D.

Dana, Benjamin, Lieutenant.
Danforth, Joshua, Lieutenant.
Daniels, Japheth, Captain.
Darby, Samuel, Major.
Davis, Ebenezer, Lieutenant, and Brigadier Quarter-Master.
Davis, James, Lieutenant.
Davis, John, Lieutenant and Adjutant.
Dean, Walter, Captain.
Dix, Nathan, Captain.
Dodge, Levi, Lieutenant.
Drew, Seth, Major.
Duffield, John, Regimental Surgeon.

E.

Eaton, Benjamin, Lieutenant.
Edwards, Thomas, Lieutenant and Judge-Advocate.
Egleston, Azariah, Lieutenant and Pay-Master.
Emerson, Nehemiah, Captain.
Emery, Ephraim, Lieutenant and Pay-Master.
Eustis, William, Hospital Surgeon.
Everett, Pelatiah, Lieutenant.
Eysandeau, William, Lieutenant.

F.

Felt, Jonathan, Captain.
Finley, James E. B., Regimental Surgeon.
Finley, Samuel, Regimental Surgeon.
Fisk, Joseph, Regimental Surgeon.
Floyd, Ebenezer, Ensign.
Foster, Elisha, Ensign.
Foster, Thomas, Lieutenant.
Fowles, John, Captain.
Freeman, Constant, Captain-Lieutenant.
Freeman, Thomas D., Lieutenant.
Frink, Samuel, Ensign.
Frost, Samuel, Captain.
Frothingham, Benjamin, Captain.
Frye, Frederick, Ensign.
Fuller, John, Captain.

G.

Gardner, James, Captain-Lieutenant.
Garrett, Andrew, Lieutenant.
George, John, Captain-Lieutenant.
Gibbs, Caleb, Major.
Gilbert, Benjamin, Lieutenant.
Goodale, Nathan, Captain.
Goodwin, F. L. B., Surgeon's Mate.
Greaton, John, Brigadier-General.
Greaton, John W., Ensign.
Greaton, Richard H., Ensign.
Green, Francis, Captain.
Greenleaf, William, Lieutenant.
Gridley, John, Captain-Lieutenant.

H.

Hall, James, Lieutenant.
Hamlin, Africa, Ensign.
Hancock, Belcher, Captain.
Hart, John, Regimental Surgeon.
Hartshorn, Thomas, Captain.
Harvey, Elisha, Captain-Lieutenant,
Haskell, Elnathan, Captain.
Haskell, Jonathan, Lieutenant.
Hastings, John, Captain.
Heath, William, Major-General.
Heywood, Benjamin, Captain.
Hildreth, William, Lieutenant.
Hill, Jeremiah, Lieutenant.
Hinds, Bartlett, Captain-Lieutenant.
Hiwell, John, Lieutenant, and Inspector of Music.
Hobby, John, Captain.
Holbrook, David, Captain.
Holden, Aaron, Captain.
Holden, Abel, Captain.
Holden, John, Lieutenant.
Holden, Levi, Lieutenant.
Holland, Ivory, Lieutenant.
Holland, Park, Lieutenant.
Hollister, Jesse, Captain.
Homans, John, Surgeon.
Hooker, Zibeon, Lieutenant.
Horton, Elisha, Ensign,
Houdin, M. G., Captain.
Howe, Richard S., Ensign.
Hull, William, Lieutenant-Colonel.
Hunt, Ephraim, Lieutenant.

Hunt, Thomas, Captain.
Hurd, John, Ensign.

I.

Ingersoll, George, Lieutenant.

J.

Jackson, Amasa, Ensign.
Jackson, Charles, Ensign.
Jackson, Daniel, Lieutenant.
Jackson, Ebenezer, Lieutenant.
Jackson, Henry, Colonel.
Jackson, Michael, Colonel.
Jackson, Michael, Lieutenant.
Jackson, Simon, Captain.
Jackson, Thomas, Captain.
Jefferds, Samuel, Lieutenant.
Johnston, John, Captain.

K.

Killam, Joseph, Captain.
King, Zebulon, Captain.
Knapp, Moses, Major.
Knowles, Charles, Captain-Lieutenant.
Knox, Henry, Major-General.

L.

Larned, Simon, Captain.
Laughton, William, Surgeon's Mate.
Leavensworth, Nathaniel, Surgeon's Mate.
Lee, Daniel, Captain.
Lee, William R., Colonel.
Leland, Joseph, Lieutenant.
Leonard, Jacob, Ensign.
Lillie, John, Captain.
Lincoln, Benjamin, Major-General.
Lincoln, Rufus, Captain.
Liswell, John, Lieutenant.
Lockwood, William, Chaplain.
Lord, Jeremiah, Ensign.
Lovell, James, Lieutenant.
Lunt, Daniel, Captain.
Lyman, Cornelius, Ensign.

M.

M'Cay, Daniel, Ensign.
McKendry, William, Lieutenant.
Marble, Henry, Lieutenant.
Mason, David, Jr., Lieutenant

Maxwell, Hugh, Lieutenant-Colonel.
Maynard, John, Lieutenant and Quarter-Master.
Maynard, Jonathan, Captain.
Maynard, William, Captain.
Means, James, Captain.
Mellish, Samuel, Lieutenant.
Miller, Jeremiah, Captain.
Miller, Joseph, Lieutenant.
Mills, John, Captain.
Mills, William, Captain.
Mooars, Benjamin, Lieutenant.
Moore, William, Captain.
Moore, William, Lieutenant.
Morgan, Benjamin, Surgeon's Mate.
Morrel, Amos, Major.
Morton, Silas, Lieutenant.
Myrick, Samuel, Lieutenant.

N.

Nason, Nathaniel, Lieutenant and Quarter-Master.
Nelson, Henry, Lieutenant.
Newhall, Ezra, Lieutenant-Colonel.
Newman, Samuel, Lieutenant.
Nicholson, Samuel, Captain in the Navy.
Nixon, Thomas, Colonel.
North, William, Captain.

O.

Oliver, Alexander, Ensign.
Oliver, Robert, Major.

P.

Pardee, Aaron, Lieutenant.
Parker, Benjamin, Lieutenant.
Parker, Elias, Lieutenant.
Paterson, John, Brigadier-General.
Peabody, Ebenezer, Lieutenant.
Peirce, Benjamin, Lieutenant.
Peirce, John, Captain-Lieutenant.
Peirce, Silas, Captain.
Perkins, William, Major.
Peters, Andrew, Lieutenant-Colonel.
Pettingill, Joseph, Major.
Phelon, Edward, Lieutenant.
Phelon, John, Lieutenant.
Phelon, Patrick, Lieutenant.

46

Pike, Benjamin, Captain.
Pope, Isaac, Major.
Popkin, John, Lieutenant-Colonel.
Porter, Benjamin Jones, Surgeon's
  Mate.
Pratt, Joel, Lieutenant.
Prescott, Joseph, Hospital Mate.
Putnam, Rufus, Brigadier-General.

R.

Randall, Thomas, Captain.
Rawson, Jeduthun, Ensign.
Reab, George, Lieutenant.
Remick, Timothy, Captain.
Rice, Nathan, Major.
Rice, Oliver, Lieutenant.
Richardson, Abijah, Regimental
  Surgeon.
Rickard, William, Lieutenant.
Ripley, Hezekiah, Lieutenant.
Rouse, Oliver, Captain.
Rowe, John, Ensign.

S.

Sampson, Crocker, Lieutenant.
Sargeant, Winthrop, Captain.
Satterlee, William, Major.
Savage, Henry, Lieutenant.
Savage, Joseph, Captain.
Sawyer, James, Ensign.
Scammell, Samuel L., Ensign.
Scott, James, Ensign.
Selden, Charles, Lieutenant.
Sever, James, Ensign.
Sewall, Henry, Captain.
Seward, Thomas, Captain.
Shaw, Samuel, Captain.
Shepherd, William, Colonel.
Shepherd, William, Ensign.
Shute, Daniel, Regimental Surgeon.
Smith, Ebenezer, Captain.
Smith, Ebenezer, Captain.
Smith, John K., Captain.
Smith, Joseph, Lieutenant.
Smith, Josiah, Lieutenant.
Smith, Simeon, Captain.
Smith, Sylvanus, Captain.
Spring, Simeon, Lieutenant.
Sprout, Ebenezer, Lieutenant-Colonel-
  Commandant.

Stacey, William, Lieutenant-Colonel.
Stafford, John R., Ensign.
Stephens, William, Captain.
Stocker, Ebenezer, Lieutenant.
Stone, Jonathan, Captain.
Stone, Nathaniel, Lieutenant.
Storer, Ebenezer, Lieutenant and
  Pay-Master.
Story, John.
Story, William, Captain.
Sumner, Job, Major.
Swan, Caleb, Ensign.

T.

Taylor, Othniel, Captain.
Taylor, Tertius, Lieutenant.
Taylor, William, Lieutenant and
  Quarter-Master.
Thacher, James, Regimental Surgeon.
Thatcher, Nathaniel, Lieutenant.
Thomas, John, Regimental Surgeon.
Thomas, Joseph, Captain.
Thomas, Thaddeus, Lieutenant-
  Colonel.
Tisdale, James, Captain.
Torrey, William, Lieutenant and
  Adjutant.
Town, Jacob, Lieutenant.
Townsend, David, Hospital Surgeon.
Treadwell, William, Captain.
Trescott, Lemuel, Major.
Trowbridge, Luther, Lieutenant.
Trotter, John, Captain.
Tucker, Joseph, Lieutenant and
  Pay-Master.
Tudor, William, Lieutenant-Colonel
  and Judge-Advocate-General.
Tupper, Anselm, Lieutenant and
  Adjutant.
Tupper, Benjamin, Colonel.
Turner, Jonathan, Captain.
Turner, Marlbray, Lieutenant.
Turner, Peleg, Lieutenant.
Turner, Thomas, Captain.

V.

Vose, Elijah, Lieutenant-Colonel
Vose, Joseph, Colonel.
Vose, Thomas, Captain.

W.

Wales, Joseph, Lieutenant.
Walker, Edward, Lieutenant and
Pay-Master.
Walker, Robert, Captain.
Wardwell, Joseph, Lieutenant.
Warren, Adriel, Lieutenant.
Warren, James, Jr., Lieutenant in
the Navy.
Warren, John, Lieutenant.
Watson, William, Captain.
Wattles, Mason, Captain.
Webb, George, Captain.
Webber, Daniel, Lieutenant.
Wellington, Elisha, Lieutenant.
Wells, Benjamin, Lieutenant.
Wells, James, Lieutenant.
Wells, Thomas, Captain.
Wesson, James, Colonel.
White, Edward, Lieutenant.

White, Haffield, Captain.
Whiting, John, Lieutenant.
Whitwell, Samuel, Surgeon.
Wild, Ebenezer, Lieutenant.
Williams, Abraham, Captain.
Williams, Ebenezer, Lieutenant.
Williams, John, Captain.
Williams, Joseph, Captain.
Williams, Robert, Lieutenant and
Pay-Master.
Wing, Jonathan, Ensign.
Winslow, John, Captain.
Woodbridge, Christopher, Captain.
Woodward, Samuel, Surgeon's Mate.

Y.

Yoeman, John, Lieutenant.

WHOLE NUMBER, 334.

THE

MASSACHUSETTS SOCIETY OF THE CINCINNATI.

1883.

OFFICERS.

President.

SAMUEL C. COBB.

Vice-President.

CHARLES D. HOMANS.

Secretary.

FRANCIS W. PALFREY.

Treasurer.

WINSLOW WARREN.

Assistant Treasurer.

GAMALIEL BRADFORD.

Assistant Secretary.

DAVID G. HASKINS, JR.

Standing Committee.

WILLIAM PERKINS.
SAMUEL K. LOTHROP.
EDWARD S. MOSELEY.
WILLIAM RAYMOND LEE.
BENJAMIN A. GOULD.
HENRY J. HUNT.

J. HUNTINGTON WOLCOTT.
CHARLES W. STOREY.
BENJAMIN H. GREENE.
ALEXANDER WILLIAMS.
J. COLLINS WARREN.
BENJAMIN LINCOLN.

MEMBERS

OF THE

MASSACHUSETTS SOCIETY OF THE CINCINNATI.

1883.

Samuel Alden.
Leonard Arnold.
S. D. Bailey.
Walter L. Bailey.
Edmund L. Baylies.
Frederic F. Baury.
Charles Upham Bell.
Stephen W. Bowles.
Gamaliel Bradford.
Robert F. Bradford.
Thomas G. Bradford.
James Bullard.
F. Prescott Bullock.
William II. Burbeck.
Thomas L. Casey.
William Chase.
Charles B. Clapp.
Samuel C. Clarke.
Samuel C. Cobb.
George H. Cooper.
Lewis C. Crocker.
Prentiss Cummings.
Charles H. Davis.
John J. Doland.
Clement Drew.
Charles M. Eaton.
John Edwards.
Nathaniel W. Emerson.
William Eustis.

Benjamin A. Gould.
Benjamin H. Greene.
David G. Haskins, Jr.
Edmund T. Hastings.
John G. Heywood.
J. Russell Hodge.
Charles D. Homans.
Henry J. Hunt.
Francis Jackson.
Alexander B. Keyes.
Gilbert C. Knapp.
Amos A. Lawrence.
Charles O. Lawton.
William Raymond Lee.
Daniel C. Lillie.
Benjamin Lincoln.
Samuel K. Lothrop.
Mansfield Lovell.
William M. Maxwell.
George A. McKendry.
John W. Moore.
Edward S. Moseley.
J. W. A. Nicholson.
Marcellus Nixon.
Edward K. O'Brien.
Francis W. Palfrey.
Henry A. Peirce.
William Perkins.
Andrew P. Perry.

John L. Peters.
John Pickering.
Josiah Pierce.
William Pitt Preble.
Nathan P. Rice.
George D. Richardson.
William H. Savage.
George A. Sawyer.
Winslow Warren Sever.
Richard T. Seward.
Daniel Shute.
Henry Knox Sikes.
William H. Smith.
John J. Soren.
Henry H. Sproat.
John T. Stoddard.
Charles W. Storey.

Edwin V. Sumner.
Charles H. Thompson.
William Torrey.
E. D. Townsend.
George C. Trumbull.
Frederick Tudor.
Joseph B. Upham.
James G. Vose.
Thomas S. Vose.
William H. Wardwell.
J. Collins Warren.
Winslow Warren.
George Peabody Wetmore.
William D. Whiting.
Charles Tidd Wild.
Alexander Williams.
J. Huntington Wolcott.

·

www.ingramcontent.com/pod-product-compliance
Lightning Source LLC
Chambersburg PA
CBHW031819090426
42739CB00008B/1338